A TEACHER'S GUIDE TO EMPOWER YOUR CHILDREN

Teach Kids to Ask Meaningful

Questions, Recognize Bias, and

Stand Up for Themselves

Thomas Rowley PhD

A TEACHERS GUIDE TO EMPOWER YOUR CHILDREN
Teach Kids to Ask Meaningful Questions, Recognize Bias, and Stand up for Themselves

ISBN: 978-1-7370353-4-3 Teacher's Guide

         978-1-7370353-2-9 e-book

         978-1-7370353-3-6   paperback edition

         978-1-7370353-5-0   hardback edition

         LCCN   2021919119

Preface

As the author of the book *EMPOWER YOUR CHILDREN- Teach kids to ask meaningful questions, recognize bias, and stand up for themselves*, I am an Advocate who believes critical thinking (CT) is important.

It is a combined obligation of both the parents and teachers to get students in the habit of discovering who wrote the material they are studying, why the author wrote it, and who was the author's intended audience. That is usually clear by reading the preface and doing at least cursory investigation into the reputation and reliability of the author(s).

This Guide provides a worksheet for each class with notes and reminders on how to utilize the basic questions with each text or article that is being covered in that lesson.

Included is a series of twenty-six worksheet pages for a two-semester schedule, teacher's notes for implementation, and time to be allocated of the class to the CT aspects.

They are two-sided pages with open spaces for teacher's notes. The first page is a Teacher Planning Page. It includes:

- Topic for the day.
- The author and their credentials.
- Why this is valuable for the student to understand and how it applies to them.
- How the teacher will develop and approach the subject: Lecture / Q&A / summary with exercises to practice application and demonstrate understanding.

K–6:

Depending on the grade level, either read the preface and explain it to the class or have the students read it to themselves. If there are students struggling with reading or speaking this is a good opportunity for them to practice. Ask for a volunteer or assign a student to read it aloud to the class.

But DO review the preface of the book with the class—it will give them a sense of why the author invested the effort to write the material and often identifies the target audience, their "avatar."

I see my role as a facilitator in encouraging teachers to become Advocates. In grade levels K–6, the teacher will be the researcher and explain The Four W's to the class.

K–7 or 8

In year/grade level 7, I recommend a weekly one-hour class period devoted to a deeper investigation of a local news story of significance.

Recommendation: For the first two sessions, the teacher selects something from the front page of the local newspaper to be the basis of the discussion. Yes, I know students probably don't read newspapers, but newspapers are online and can be read. The point of the exercise is to get young people to be aware of what is going on around them, in their neighborhood, community, and region and in the world—which is so connected now with their handheld devices.

For the next few weeks, depending on the skill levels of their students, the teacher should provide three optional topics drawn from current events, news stories, or a topic related to the subject material specifically for the students to select to be the basis of THEIR research to answer the questions.

College or University:

In the first year of college the author recommends developing a semester course of at least two credit hours so that incoming students learn and comprehend the best practices to evaluate reports and academic studies they will be encountering and using as the basis of their own research papers or thesis.

The author of *EMPOWER YOUR CHILDREN* taught a business and professional speaking course for a decade which commenced with exposing his students to these critical thinking skills development in the first third of the course. Feedback from his students was overwhelmingly positive. They disclosed that the material and procedures learned in his class had enhanced their subsequent studies and the classroom presentations they made.

The author encourages other professors to read the book for which this Guide has been produced. The publisher of the book has developed several online training courses and live workshops including slides and additional materials that are available for purchase at a discount to qualified educational professionals. I invite you to visit the website www.blameitonnam.com/courses to discover what is currently available and if there is a workshop program that is convenient for you.

The goal is for the teacher and students to become proficient in evaluating the sources of information and assessing the reliability and accuracy of the reporting to be able to use verifiable facts in their personal decision-making and how they choose to react and respond to the information.

The back page serves as a self-evaluation of the effectiveness of the exercise:

- Notes on student responses (positive/neutral /negative).
- What went well.
- What didn't go as planned/anticipated.
- What the teacher would do differently next time to improve student involvement, understanding, and growth.

My admiration and appreciation to each of you for your efforts in improving the development of useful life skills in your students. Skills that will empower them to become successful, productive adults. Your life and theirs will be better for it.

Tom Rowley

Panama City, Panama

November 2021

A Teacher's Guide

Introduction and Overview

The goal of this Guide is to facilitate a simple way to incorporate into your daily and weekly lesson plans an easy method to introduce the concepts of becoming a critical thinker to your students which relates directly to the subject they are learning. Start with the earliest classes.

If you've read my book, *EMPOWER YOUR CHILDREN*, you may have gone online to our web page and received the gift of the Four W's:

1. Says Who?
2. Why should I care?
3. Why should I believe you?
4. Where's the proof?

We all need to encourage the natural curiosity of children and instill the habit of asking those four questions of the information we are presented. Those questions are answered by asking: Who wrote it? When was it published? What is the writer's experience or expertise that qualified them to be an "authority" on the topic? What was the author's goal in writing the material? Who was the author's intended audience?

My WHY? I saw public officials proposing a series of life-changing decisions as solutions to problems and concluded that politics aside, there has been a failure in education to provide the critical thinking skills for people to make well-informed choices. I believe that there is a relatively simple solution to these complex problems. Note I didn't say easy solution. The problem has many layers and players. It is complex. The solution is not complex, but it is complicated. There are many moving—or in some cases frozen—parts that need to be changed.

And you apparently agree or you wouldn't have invested to become one of the cadre of **Teacher Advocates** who want to incorporate these techniques in your toolkit and use them in a casual, nonthreatening way in building the habit in your students.

My WHAT is the goal for the addition of training in critical thinking skills to the curriculum of K–12 and freshman year of college. Each student needs to learn to be a **respectful skeptic**.

My HOW is I believe we should create a cadre of thousands of Apprentices and Challengers. But to have any expectation of a positive change in public education, I am convinced we need to have thousands of **Teacher Advocates**. It starts with a thousand Challengers at the individual level. Home. Family. School. Parents and grandparents who demonstrate critical thinking when discussing the events of the day and asking what their children are studying and what their teachers are telling them.

Teachers and counselors hold a respected position in young peoples' lives. They are looked up to as role models. Teachers who daily demonstrate those skills in K–12 classroom assignments will have an impact on their students that will last a lifetime— long past their graduation. They may never forget that special teacher, the one who encouraged them to ask the Four W's and demonstrated the utility and value of asking questions.

Included in this movement are the coaches and guides in youth organizations, sports activities, and even religious activities for young people. When those leaders demonstrate careful thinking and analyses based on facts it will anchor the concept in those young minds for a lifetime.

Your students will learn to make daily choices based on facts. When the students do that, they will have a realistic vision of what is the likely result from the everyday choices each of us make, from what to eat and wear to who to befriend and emulate. They will become the productive, successful adults all parents and teachers desire for the young people they are responsible for raising.

Teacher Advocates hold a unique position to change lives for the better. Most of you already know that, but let me encourage and congratulate you for taking these steps to introduce fact-finding skills to the children in your care.

Effective, long-lasting change first has to be personal. We must start at home plate. You and the student's parents are partners in this worthy endeavor. Encourage your students to talk with their parents about what they are learning and how you are helping them learn HOW to learn, not just what to know to get promoted to the next level.

Lesson Plan For Incorporating Critical Thinking

Class/week No:_____ Grade Level:_____

Topic of the class:_____

Why this is valuable for the student to understand: WIFM (What's In It For Me).

_____

_____

How the teacher will develop and approach the subject: Lecture/Q&A/summary with exercises to practice application and demo understanding.

_____

_____

Supporting reading material provided the students:

_____

_____

Author:_____

Author's education and experience:_____

Author's reputation and public profile: _____

Questions as the students work the material for the day (The students WIFM):

Why did the author include this material?

_____

How does this material integrate with other material/readings/presentations they have had?

_____

What is the value to the student to learn about this?

_____

How can the student incorporate the material into their daily lives?

_____

How does this material provide a skill they can use to make better choices?

_____

Post-class Evaluation Of The Effectiveness Of The Exercise

On a scale of 1 to 5 how would you rate the overall activity and learning experience for the students (1 being poor or very little, 5 being excellent)?

1   2   3   4   5

Did the exercise increase student involvement and action in the lesson?

_____

_____

Did the information about the author and their background invite active questions and discussion by the students?

_____

_____

Did the students see the relationship between today's class activities and other classes or courses by other teachers?

_____

_____

Did the students demonstrate how they could apply what they were hearing or discussing in their day-to-day activities?

_____

_____

What would you, the teacher, do differently next time?

_____

_____

_____

_____

Lesson Plan For Incorporating Critical Thinking

Class/week No:_____ Grade Level:_____

Topic of the class:_____

Why this is valuable for the student to understand: WIFM (What's In It For Me).

_____

_____

How the teacher will develop and approach the subject: Lecture/Q&A/summary with exercises to practice application and demo understanding.

_____

_____

Supporting reading material provided the students:

_____

_____

Author:_____

Author's education and experience:_____

Author's reputation and public profile: _____

Questions as the students work the material for the day (The students WIFM):

Why did the author include this material?

_____

How does this material integrate with other material/readings/presentations they have had?

_____

What is the value to the student to learn about this?

_____

How can the student incorporate the material into their daily lives?

_____

How does this material provide a skill they can use to make better choices?

_____

Post-class Evaluation Of The Effectiveness Of The Exercise

On a scale of 1 to 5 how would you rate the overall activity and learning experience for the students (1 being poor or very little, 5 being excellent)?

1   2   3   4   5

Did the exercise increase student involvement and action in the lesson?
_____
_____

Did the information about the author and their background invite active questions and discussion by the students?
_____
_____

Did the students see the relationship between today's class activities and other classes or courses by other teachers?
_____
_____

Did the students demonstrate how they could apply what they were hearing or discussing in their day-to-day activities?
_____
_____

What would you, the teacher, do differently next time?
_____
_____
_____
_____

Lesson Plan For Incorporating Critical Thinking

Class/week No:_____ Grade Level:_____

Topic of the class:_____

Why this is valuable for the student to understand: WIFM (What's In It For Me).

_____

_____

How the teacher will develop and approach the subject: Lecture/Q&A/summary with exercises to practice application and demo understanding.

_____

_____

Supporting reading material provided the students:

_____

_____

Author:_____

Author's education and experience:_____

Author's reputation and public profile: _____

Questions as the students work the material for the day (The students WIFM):

Why did the author include this material?

_____

How does this material integrate with other material/readings/presentations they have had?

_____

What is the value to the student to learn about this?

_____

How can the student incorporate the material into their daily lives?

_____

How does this material provide a skill they can use to make better choices?

_____

Post-class Evaluation Of The Effectiveness Of The Exercise

On a scale of 1 to 5 how would you rate the overall activity and learning experience for the students (1 being poor or very little, 5 being excellent)?

1   2   3   4   5

Did the exercise increase student involvement and action in the lesson?
_____
_____

Did the information about the author and their background invite active questions and discussion by the students?
_____
_____

Did the students see the relationship between today's class activities and other classes or courses by other teachers?
_____
_____

Did the students demonstrate how they could apply what they were hearing or discussing in their day-to-day activities?
_____
_____

What would you, the teacher, do differently next time?
_____
_____
_____
_____

Lesson Plan For Incorporating Critical Thinking

Class/week No:_____ Grade Level:_____

Topic of the class:_____

Why this is valuable for the student to understand: WIFM (What's In It For Me).

_____

_____

How the teacher will develop and approach the subject: Lecture/Q&A/summary with exercises to practice application and demo understanding.

_____

_____

Supporting reading material provided the students:

_____

_____

Author:_____

Author's education and experience:_____

Author's reputation and public profile: _____

Questions as the students work the material for the day (The students WIFM):

Why did the author include this material?

_____

How does this material integrate with other material/readings/presentations they have had?

_____

What is the value to the student to learn about this?

_____

How can the student incorporate the material into their daily lives?

_____

How does this material provide a skill they can use to make better choices?

_____

Post-class Evaluation Of The Effectiveness Of The Exercise

On a scale of 1 to 5 how would you rate the overall activity and learning experience for the students (1 being poor or very little, 5 being excellent)?

1   2   3   4   5

Did the exercise increase student involvement and action in the lesson?

_____

_____

Did the information about the author and their background invite active questions and discussion by the students?

_____

_____

Did the students see the relationship between today's class activities and other classes or courses by other teachers?

_____

_____

Did the students demonstrate how they could apply what they were hearing or discussing in their day-to-day activities?

_____

_____

What would you, the teacher, do differently next time?

_____

_____

_____

_____

© 2021 Empower Your Children Teacher's Guide

Lesson Plan For Incorporating Critical Thinking

Class/week No:_____ Grade Level:_____

Topic of the class:_____

Why this is valuable for the student to understand: WIFM (What's In It For Me).

_____

_____

How the teacher will develop and approach the subject: Lecture/Q&A/summary with exercises to practice application and demo understanding.

_____

_____

Supporting reading material provided the students:

_____

_____

Author:_____

Author's education and experience:_____

Author's reputation and public profile: _____

Questions as the students work the material for the day (The students WIFM):

Why did the author include this material?

_____

How does this material integrate with other material/readings/presentations they have had?

_____

What is the value to the student to learn about this?

_____

How can the student incorporate the material into their daily lives?

_____

How does this material provide a skill they can use to make better choices?

_____

Post-class Evaluation Of The Effectiveness Of The Exercise

On a scale of 1 to 5 how would you rate the overall activity and learning experience for the students (1 being poor or very little, 5 being excellent)?

1   2   3   4   5

Did the exercise increase student involvement and action in the lesson?

_____

_____

Did the information about the author and their background invite active questions and discussion by the students?

_____

_____

Did the students see the relationship between today's class activities and other classes or courses by other teachers?

_____

_____

Did the students demonstrate how they could apply what they were hearing or discussing in their day-to-day activities?

_____

_____

What would you, the teacher, do differently next time?

_____

_____

_____

_____

Lesson Plan For Incorporating Critical Thinking

Class/week No:_____ Grade Level:_____

Topic of the class:_____

Why this is valuable for the student to understand: WIFM (What's In It For Me).

_____

_____

How the teacher will develop and approach the subject: Lecture/Q&A/summary with exercises to practice application and demo understanding.

_____

_____

Supporting reading material provided the students:

_____

_____

Author:_____

Author's education and experience:_____

Author's reputation and public profile: _____

Questions as the students work the material for the day (The students WIFM):

Why did the author include this material?

_____

How does this material integrate with other material/readings/presentations they have had?

_____

What is the value to the student to learn about this?

_____

How can the student incorporate the material into their daily lives?

_____

How does this material provide a skill they can use to make better choices?

_____

Post-class Evaluation Of The Effectiveness Of The Exercise

On a scale of 1 to 5 how would you rate the overall activity and learning experience for the students (1 being poor or very little, 5 being excellent)?

1   2   3   4   5

Did the exercise increase student involvement and action in the lesson?

_____

_____

Did the information about the author and their background invite active questions and discussion by the students?

_____

_____

Did the students see the relationship between today's class activities and other classes or courses by other teachers?

_____

_____

Did the students demonstrate how they could apply what they were hearing or discussing in their day-to-day activities?

_____

_____

What would you, the teacher, do differently next time?

_____

_____

_____

_____

Lesson Plan For Incorporating Critical Thinking

Class/week No:_____ Grade Level:_____

Topic of the class:_____

Why this is valuable for the student to understand: WIFM (What's In It For Me).

_____

_____

How the teacher will develop and approach the subject: Lecture/Q&A/summary with exercises to practice application and demo understanding.

_____

_____

Supporting reading material provided the students:

_____

_____

Author:_____

Author's education and experience:_____

Author's reputation and public profile: _____

Questions as the students work the material for the day (The students WIFM):

Why did the author include this material?

_____

How does this material integrate with other material/readings/presentations they have had?

_____

What is the value to the student to learn about this?

_____

How can the student incorporate the material into their daily lives?

_____

How does this material provide a skill they can use to make better choices?

_____

Post-class Evaluation Of The Effectiveness Of The Exercise

On a scale of 1 to 5 how would you rate the overall activity and learning experience for the students (1 being poor or very little, 5 being excellent)?

1   2   3   4   5

Did the exercise increase student involvement and action in the lesson?

_____

_____

Did the information about the author and their background invite active questions and discussion by the students?

_____

_____

Did the students see the relationship between today's class activities and other classes or courses by other teachers?

_____

_____

Did the students demonstrate how they could apply what they were hearing or discussing in their day-to-day activities?

_____

_____

What would you, the teacher, do differently next time?

_____

_____

_____

_____

Lesson Plan For Incorporating Critical Thinking

Class/week No:_____ Grade Level:_____

Topic of the class:_____

Why this is valuable for the student to understand: WIFM (What's In It For Me).

_____

_____

How the teacher will develop and approach the subject: Lecture/Q&A/summary with exercises to practice application and demo understanding.

_____

_____

Supporting reading material provided the students:

_____

_____

Author:_____

Author's education and experience:_____

Author's reputation and public profile: _____

Questions as the students work the material for the day (The students WIFM):

Why did the author include this material?

_____

How does this material integrate with other material/readings/presentations they have had?

_____

What is the value to the student to learn about this?

_____

How can the student incorporate the material into their daily lives?

_____

How does this material provide a skill they can use to make better choices?

_____

Post-class Evaluation Of The Effectiveness Of The Exercise

On a scale of 1 to 5 how would you rate the overall activity and learning experience for the students (1 being poor or very little, 5 being excellent)?

1   2   3   4   5

Did the exercise increase student involvement and action in the lesson?

_____

_____

Did the information about the author and their background invite active questions and discussion by the students?

_____

_____

Did the students see the relationship between today's class activities and other classes or courses by other teachers?

_____

_____

Did the students demonstrate how they could apply what they were hearing or discussing in their day-to-day activities?

_____

_____

What would you, the teacher, do differently next time?

_____

_____

_____

_____

Lesson Plan For Incorporating Critical Thinking

Class/week No:_____ Grade Level:_____

Topic of the class:_____

Why this is valuable for the student to understand: WIFM (What's In It For Me).

_____

_____

How the teacher will develop and approach the subject: Lecture/Q&A/summary with exercises to practice application and demo understanding.

_____

_____

Supporting reading material provided the students:

_____

_____

Author:_____

Author's education and experience:_____

Author's reputation and public profile: _____

Questions as the students work the material for the day (The students WIFM):

Why did the author include this material?

_____

How does this material integrate with other material/readings/presentations they have had?

_____

What is the value to the student to learn about this?

_____

How can the student incorporate the material into their daily lives?

_____

How does this material provide a skill they can use to make better choices?

_____

Post-class Evaluation Of The Effectiveness Of The Exercise

On a scale of 1 to 5 how would you rate the overall activity and learning experience for the students (1 being poor or very little, 5 being excellent)?

1   2   3   4   5

Did the exercise increase student involvement and action in the lesson?

_____

_____

Did the information about the author and their background invite active questions and discussion by the students?

_____

_____

Did the students see the relationship between today's class activities and other classes or courses by other teachers?

_____

_____

Did the students demonstrate how they could apply what they were hearing or discussing in their day-to-day activities?

_____

_____

What would you, the teacher, do differently next time?

_____

_____

_____

_____

Lesson Plan For Incorporating Critical Thinking

Class/week No:_____ Grade Level:_____

Topic of the class:_____

Why this is valuable for the student to understand: WIFM (What's In It For Me).

_____

_____

How the teacher will develop and approach the subject: Lecture/Q&A/summary with exercises to practice application and demo understanding.

_____

_____

Supporting reading material provided the students:

_____

_____

Author:_____

Author's education and experience:_____

Author's reputation and public profile: _____

Questions as the students work the material for the day (The students WIFM):

Why did the author include this material?

_____

How does this material integrate with other material/readings/presentations they have had?

_____

What is the value to the student to learn about this?

_____

How can the student incorporate the material into their daily lives?

_____

How does this material provide a skill they can use to make better choices?

_____

Post-class Evaluation Of The Effectiveness Of The Exercise

On a scale of 1 to 5 how would you rate the overall activity and learning experience for the students (1 being poor or very little, 5 being excellent)?

1   2   3   4   5

Did the exercise increase student involvement and action in the lesson?
_____
_____

Did the information about the author and their background invite active questions and discussion by the students?
_____
_____

Did the students see the relationship between today's class activities and other classes or courses by other teachers?
_____
_____

Did the students demonstrate how they could apply what they were hearing or discussing in their day-to-day activities?
_____
_____

What would you, the teacher, do differently next time?
_____
_____
_____
_____

Lesson Plan For Incorporating Critical Thinking

Class/week No:_____ Grade Level:_____

Topic of the class:_____

Why this is valuable for the student to understand: WIFM (What's In It For Me).

_____

_____

How the teacher will develop and approach the subject: Lecture/Q&A/summary with exercises to practice application and demo understanding.

_____

_____

Supporting reading material provided the students:

_____

_____

Author:_____

Author's education and experience:_____

Author's reputation and public profile: _____

Questions as the students work the material for the day (The students WIFM):

Why did the author include this material?

_____

How does this material integrate with other material/readings/presentations they have had?

_____

What is the value to the student to learn about this?

_____

How can the student incorporate the material into their daily lives?

_____

How does this material provide a skill they can use to make better choices?

_____

Post-class Evaluation Of The Effectiveness Of The Exercise

On a scale of 1 to 5 how would you rate the overall activity and learning experience for the students (1 being poor or very little, 5 being excellent)?

1   2   3   4   5

Did the exercise increase student involvement and action in the lesson?
_____
_____

Did the information about the author and their background invite active questions and discussion by the students?
_____
_____

Did the students see the relationship between today's class activities and other classes or courses by other teachers?
_____
_____

Did the students demonstrate how they could apply what they were hearing or discussing in their day-to-day activities?
_____
_____

What would you, the teacher, do differently next time?
_____
_____
_____
_____

Lesson Plan For Incorporating Critical Thinking

Class/week No:_____ Grade Level:_____

Topic of the class:_____

Why this is valuable for the student to understand: WIFM (What's In It For Me).

_____

_____

How the teacher will develop and approach the subject: Lecture/Q&A/summary with exercises to practice application and demo understanding.

_____

_____

Supporting reading material provided the students:

_____

_____

Author:_____

Author's education and experience:_____

Author's reputation and public profile: _____

Questions as the students work the material for the day (The students WIFM):

Why did the author include this material?

_____

How does this material integrate with other material/readings/presentations they have had?

_____

What is the value to the student to learn about this?

_____

How can the student incorporate the material into their daily lives?

_____

How does this material provide a skill they can use to make better choices?

_____

Post-class Evaluation Of The Effectiveness Of The Exercise

On a scale of 1 to 5 how would you rate the overall activity and learning experience for the students (1 being poor or very little, 5 being excellent)?

1   2   3   4   5

Did the exercise increase student involvement and action in the lesson?
_____
_____

Did the information about the author and their background invite active questions and discussion by the students?
_____
_____

Did the students see the relationship between today's class activities and other classes or courses by other teachers?
_____
_____

Did the students demonstrate how they could apply what they were hearing or discussing in their day-to-day activities?
_____
_____

What would you, the teacher, do differently next time?
_____
_____
_____
_____

Lesson Plan For Incorporating Critical Thinking

Class/week No:_____ Grade Level:_____

Topic of the class:_____

Why this is valuable for the student to understand: WIFM (What's In It For Me).

_____

_____

How the teacher will develop and approach the subject: Lecture/Q&A/summary with exercises to practice application and demo understanding.

_____

_____

Supporting reading material provided the students:

_____

_____

Author:_____

Author's education and experience:_____

Author's reputation and public profile: _____

Questions as the students work the material for the day (The students WIFM):

Why did the author include this material?

_____

How does this material integrate with other material/readings/presentations they have had?

_____

What is the value to the student to learn about this?

_____

How can the student incorporate the material into their daily lives?

_____

How does this material provide a skill they can use to make better choices?

_____

Post-class Evaluation Of The Effectiveness Of The Exercise

On a scale of 1 to 5 how would you rate the overall activity and learning experience for the students (1 being poor or very little, 5 being excellent)?

1   2   3   4   5

Did the exercise increase student involvement and action in the lesson?

_____

_____

Did the information about the author and their background invite active questions and discussion by the students?

_____

_____

Did the students see the relationship between today's class activities and other classes or courses by other teachers?

_____

_____

Did the students demonstrate how they could apply what they were hearing or discussing in their day-to-day activities?

_____

_____

What would you, the teacher, do differently next time?

_____

_____

_____

_____

Lesson Plan For Incorporating Critical Thinking

Class/week No:_____ Grade Level:_____

Topic of the class:_____

Why this is valuable for the student to understand: WIFM (What's In It For Me).

_____

_____

How the teacher will develop and approach the subject: Lecture/Q&A/summary with exercises to practice application and demo understanding.

_____

_____

Supporting reading material provided the students:

_____

_____

Author:_____

Author's education and experience:_____

Author's reputation and public profile: _____

Questions as the students work the material for the day (The students WIFM):

Why did the author include this material?

_____

How does this material integrate with other material/readings/presentations they have had?

_____

What is the value to the student to learn about this?

_____

How can the student incorporate the material into their daily lives?

_____

How does this material provide a skill they can use to make better choices?

_____

Post-class Evaluation Of The Effectiveness Of The Exercise

On a scale of 1 to 5 how would you rate the overall activity and learning experience for the students (1 being poor or very little, 5 being excellent)?

1   2   3   4   5

Did the exercise increase student involvement and action in the lesson?
_____
_____

Did the information about the author and their background invite active questions and discussion by the students?
_____
_____

Did the students see the relationship between today's class activities and other classes or courses by other teachers?
_____
_____

Did the students demonstrate how they could apply what they were hearing or discussing in their day-to-day activities?
_____
_____

What would you, the teacher, do differently next time?
_____
_____
_____
_____

Lesson Plan For Incorporating Critical Thinking

Class/week No:_____ Grade Level:_____

Topic of the class:_____

Why this is valuable for the student to understand: WIFM (What's In It For Me).

_____

_____

How the teacher will develop and approach the subject: Lecture/Q&A/summary with exercises to practice application and demo understanding.

_____

_____

Supporting reading material provided the students:

_____

_____

Author:_____

Author's education and experience:_____

Author's reputation and public profile: _____

Questions as the students work the material for the day (The students WIFM):

Why did the author include this material?

_____

How does this material integrate with other material/readings/presentations they have had?

_____

What is the value to the student to learn about this?

_____

How can the student incorporate the material into their daily lives?

_____

How does this material provide a skill they can use to make better choices?

_____

Post-class Evaluation Of The Effectiveness Of The Exercise

On a scale of 1 to 5 how would you rate the overall activity and learning experience for the students (1 being poor or very little, 5 being excellent)?

1   2   3   4   5

Did the exercise increase student involvement and action in the lesson?

_____

_____

Did the information about the author and their background invite active questions and discussion by the students?

_____

_____

Did the students see the relationship between today's class activities and other classes or courses by other teachers?

_____

_____

Did the students demonstrate how they could apply what they were hearing or discussing in their day-to-day activities?

_____

_____

What would you, the teacher, do differently next time?

_____

_____

_____

_____

Lesson Plan For Incorporating Critical Thinking

Class/week No:_____ Grade Level:_____

Topic of the class:_____

Why this is valuable for the student to understand: WIFM (What's In It For Me).

_____

_____

How the teacher will develop and approach the subject: Lecture/Q&A/summary with exercises to practice application and demo understanding.

_____

_____

Supporting reading material provided the students:

_____

_____

Author:_____

Author's education and experience:_____

Author's reputation and public profile: _____

Questions as the students work the material for the day (The students WIFM):

Why did the author include this material?

_____

How does this material integrate with other material/readings/presentations they have had?

_____

What is the value to the student to learn about this?

_____

How can the student incorporate the material into their daily lives?

_____

How does this material provide a skill they can use to make better choices?

_____

Post-class Evaluation Of The Effectiveness Of The Exercise

On a scale of 1 to 5 how would you rate the overall activity and learning experience for the students (1 being poor or very little, 5 being excellent)?

1   2   3   4   5

Did the exercise increase student involvement and action in the lesson?
_____
_____

Did the information about the author and their background invite active questions and discussion by the students?
_____
_____

Did the students see the relationship between today's class activities and other classes or courses by other teachers?
_____
_____

Did the students demonstrate how they could apply what they were hearing or discussing in their day-to-day activities?
_____
_____

What would you, the teacher, do differently next time?
_____
_____
_____
_____

Lesson Plan For Incorporating Critical Thinking

Class/week No:_____ Grade Level:_____

Topic of the class:_____

Why this is valuable for the student to understand: WIFM (What's In It For Me).

_____

_____

How the teacher will develop and approach the subject: Lecture/Q&A/summary with exercises to practice application and demo understanding.

_____

_____

Supporting reading material provided the students:

_____

_____

Author:_____

Author's education and experience:_____

Author's reputation and public profile: _____

Questions as the students work the material for the day (The students WIFM):

Why did the author include this material?

_____

How does this material integrate with other material/readings/presentations they have had?

_____

What is the value to the student to learn about this?

_____

How can the student incorporate the material into their daily lives?

_____

How does this material provide a skill they can use to make better choices?

_____

Post-class Evaluation Of The Effectiveness Of The Exercise

On a scale of 1 to 5 how would you rate the overall activity and learning experience for the students (1 being poor or very little, 5 being excellent)?

1   2   3   4   5

Did the exercise increase student involvement and action in the lesson?
_____
_____

Did the information about the author and their background invite active questions and discussion by the students?
_____
_____

Did the students see the relationship between today's class activities and other classes or courses by other teachers?
_____
_____

Did the students demonstrate how they could apply what they were hearing or discussing in their day-to-day activities?
_____
_____

What would you, the teacher, do differently next time?
_____
_____
_____
_____

Lesson Plan For Incorporating Critical Thinking

Class/week No:_____ Grade Level:_____

Topic of the class:_____

Why this is valuable for the student to understand: WIFM (What's In It For Me).

_____

_____

How the teacher will develop and approach the subject: Lecture/Q&A/summary with exercises to practice application and demo understanding.

_____

_____

Supporting reading material provided the students:

_____

_____

Author:_____

Author's education and experience:_____

Author's reputation and public profile: _____

Questions as the students work the material for the day (The students WIFM):

Why did the author include this material?

_____

How does this material integrate with other material/readings/presentations they have had?

_____

What is the value to the student to learn about this?

_____

How can the student incorporate the material into their daily lives?

_____

How does this material provide a skill they can use to make better choices?

_____

Post-class Evaluation Of The Effectiveness Of The Exercise

On a scale of 1 to 5 how would you rate the overall activity and learning experience for the students (1 being poor or very little, 5 being excellent)?

1   2   3   4   5

Did the exercise increase student involvement and action in the lesson?
_____

_____

Did the information about the author and their background invite active questions and discussion by the students?
_____

_____

Did the students see the relationship between today's class activities and other classes or courses by other teachers?
_____

_____

Did the students demonstrate how they could apply what they were hearing or discussing in their day-to-day activities?
_____

_____

What would you, the teacher, do differently next time?
_____

_____

_____

_____

Lesson Plan For Incorporating Critical Thinking

Class/week No:_____ Grade Level:_____

Topic of the class:_____

Why this is valuable for the student to understand: WIFM (What's In It For Me).

_____

_____

How the teacher will develop and approach the subject: Lecture/Q&A/summary with exercises to practice application and demo understanding.

_____

_____

Supporting reading material provided the students:

_____

_____

Author:_____

Author's education and experience:_____

Author's reputation and public profile: _____

Questions as the students work the material for the day (The students WIFM):

Why did the author include this material?

_____

How does this material integrate with other material/readings/presentations they have had?

_____

What is the value to the student to learn about this?

_____

How can the student incorporate the material into their daily lives?

_____

How does this material provide a skill they can use to make better choices?

_____

Post-class Evaluation Of The Effectiveness Of The Exercise

On a scale of 1 to 5 how would you rate the overall activity and learning experience for the students (1 being poor or very little, 5 being excellent)?

1   2   3   4   5

Did the exercise increase student involvement and action in the lesson?
_____
_____

Did the information about the author and their background invite active questions and discussion by the students?
_____
_____

Did the students see the relationship between today's class activities and other classes or courses by other teachers?
_____
_____

Did the students demonstrate how they could apply what they were hearing or discussing in their day-to-day activities?
_____
_____

What would you, the teacher, do differently next time?
_____
_____
_____
_____

Lesson Plan For Incorporating Critical Thinking

Class/week No:_____ Grade Level:_____

Topic of the class:_____

Why this is valuable for the student to understand: WIFM (What's In It For Me).

_____

_____

How the teacher will develop and approach the subject: Lecture/Q&A/summary with exercises to practice application and demo understanding.

_____

_____

Supporting reading material provided the students:

_____

_____

Author:_____

Author's education and experience:_____

Author's reputation and public profile: _____

Questions as the students work the material for the day (The students WIFM):

Why did the author include this material?

_____

How does this material integrate with other material/readings/presentations they have had?

_____

What is the value to the student to learn about this?

_____

How can the student incorporate the material into their daily lives?

_____

How does this material provide a skill they can use to make better choices?

_____

Post-class Evaluation Of The Effectiveness Of The Exercise

On a scale of 1 to 5 how would you rate the overall activity and learning experience for the students (1 being poor or very little, 5 being excellent)?

1   2   3   4   5

Did the exercise increase student involvement and action in the lesson?
_____
_____

Did the information about the author and their background invite active questions and discussion by the students?
_____
_____

Did the students see the relationship between today's class activities and other classes or courses by other teachers?
_____
_____

Did the students demonstrate how they could apply what they were hearing or discussing in their day-to-day activities?
_____
_____

What would you, the teacher, do differently next time?
_____
_____
_____
_____

Lesson Plan For Incorporating Critical Thinking

Class/week No:_____ Grade Level:_____

Topic of the class:_____

Why this is valuable for the student to understand: WIFM (What's In It For Me).

_____

_____

How the teacher will develop and approach the subject: Lecture/Q&A/summary with exercises to practice application and demo understanding.

_____

_____

Supporting reading material provided the students:

_____

_____

Author:_____

Author's education and experience:_____

Author's reputation and public profile: _____

Questions as the students work the material for the day (The students WIFM):

Why did the author include this material?

_____

How does this material integrate with other material/readings/presentations they have had?

_____

What is the value to the student to learn about this?

_____

How can the student incorporate the material into their daily lives?

_____

How does this material provide a skill they can use to make better choices?

_____

Post-class Evaluation Of The Effectiveness Of The Exercise

On a scale of 1 to 5 how would you rate the overall activity and learning experience for the students (1 being poor or very little, 5 being excellent)?

1   2   3   4   5

Did the exercise increase student involvement and action in the lesson?

_____

_____

Did the information about the author and their background invite active questions and discussion by the students?

_____

_____

Did the students see the relationship between today's class activities and other classes or courses by other teachers?

_____

_____

Did the students demonstrate how they could apply what they were hearing or discussing in their day-to-day activities?

_____

_____

What would you, the teacher, do differently next time?

_____

_____

_____

_____

Lesson Plan For Incorporating Critical Thinking

Class/week No:_____ Grade Level:_____

Topic of the class:_____

Why this is valuable for the student to understand: WIFM (What's In It For Me).

_____

_____

How the teacher will develop and approach the subject: Lecture/Q&A/summary with exercises to practice application and demo understanding.

_____

_____

Supporting reading material provided the students:

_____

_____

Author:_____

Author's education and experience:_____

Author's reputation and public profile: _____

Questions as the students work the material for the day (The students WIFM):

Why did the author include this material?

_____

How does this material integrate with other material/readings/presentations they have had?

_____

What is the value to the student to learn about this?

_____

How can the student incorporate the material into their daily lives?

_____

How does this material provide a skill they can use to make better choices?

_____

Post-class Evaluation Of The Effectiveness Of The Exercise

On a scale of 1 to 5 how would you rate the overall activity and learning experience for the students (1 being poor or very little, 5 being excellent)?

1   2   3   4   5

Did the exercise increase student involvement and action in the lesson?
_____
_____

Did the information about the author and their background invite active questions and discussion by the students?
_____
_____

Did the students see the relationship between today's class activities and other classes or courses by other teachers?
_____
_____

Did the students demonstrate how they could apply what they were hearing or discussing in their day-to-day activities?
_____
_____

What would you, the teacher, do differently next time?
_____
_____
_____
_____

Lesson Plan For Incorporating Critical Thinking

Class/week No:_____ Grade Level:_____

Topic of the class:_____

Why this is valuable for the student to understand: WIFM (What's In It For Me).

_____

_____

How the teacher will develop and approach the subject: Lecture/Q&A/summary with exercises to practice application and demo understanding.

_____

_____

Supporting reading material provided the students:

_____

_____

Author:_____

Author's education and experience:_____

Author's reputation and public profile: _____

Questions as the students work the material for the day (The students WIFM):

Why did the author include this material?

_____

How does this material integrate with other material/readings/presentations they have had?

_____

What is the value to the student to learn about this?

_____

How can the student incorporate the material into their daily lives?

_____

How does this material provide a skill they can use to make better choices?

_____

Post-class Evaluation Of The Effectiveness Of The Exercise

On a scale of 1 to 5 how would you rate the overall activity and learning experience for the students (1 being poor or very little, 5 being excellent)?

1   2   3   4   5

Did the exercise increase student involvement and action in the lesson?

_____

_____

Did the information about the author and their background invite active questions and discussion by the students?

_____

_____

Did the students see the relationship between today's class activities and other classes or courses by other teachers?

_____

_____

Did the students demonstrate how they could apply what they were hearing or discussing in their day-to-day activities?

_____

_____

What would you, the teacher, do differently next time?

_____

_____

_____

_____

Lesson Plan For Incorporating Critical Thinking

Class/week No:_____ Grade Level:_____

Topic of the class:_____

Why this is valuable for the student to understand: WIFM (What's In It For Me).

_____

_____

How the teacher will develop and approach the subject: Lecture/Q&A/summary with exercises to practice application and demo understanding.

_____

_____

Supporting reading material provided the students:

_____

_____

Author:_____

Author's education and experience:_____

Author's reputation and public profile: _____

Questions as the students work the material for the day (The students WIFM):

Why did the author include this material?

_____

How does this material integrate with other material/readings/presentations they have had?

_____

What is the value to the student to learn about this?

_____

How can the student incorporate the material into their daily lives?

_____

How does this material provide a skill they can use to make better choices?

_____

Post-class Evaluation Of The Effectiveness Of The Exercise

On a scale of 1 to 5 how would you rate the overall activity and learning experience for the students (1 being poor or very little, 5 being excellent)?

1   2   3   4   5

Did the exercise increase student involvement and action in the lesson?

_____

_____

Did the information about the author and their background invite active questions and discussion by the students?

_____

_____

Did the students see the relationship between today's class activities and other classes or courses by other teachers?

_____

_____

Did the students demonstrate how they could apply what they were hearing or discussing in their day-to-day activities?

_____

_____

What would you, the teacher, do differently next time?

_____

_____

_____

Lesson Plan For Incorporating Critical Thinking

Class/week No:_____ Grade Level:_____

Topic of the class:_____

Why this is valuable for the student to understand: WIFM (What's In It For Me).

_____

_____

How the teacher will develop and approach the subject: Lecture/Q&A/summary with exercises to practice application and demo understanding.

_____

_____

Supporting reading material provided the students:

_____

_____

Author:_____

Author's education and experience:_____

Author's reputation and public profile: _____

Questions as the students work the material for the day (The students WIFM):

Why did the author include this material?

_____

How does this material integrate with other material/readings/presentations they have had?

_____

What is the value to the student to learn about this?

_____

How can the student incorporate the material into their daily lives?

_____

How does this material provide a skill they can use to make better choices?

_____

Post-class Evaluation Of The Effectiveness Of The Exercise

On a scale of 1 to 5 how would you rate the overall activity and learning experience for the students (1 being poor or very little, 5 being excellent)?

1   2   3   4   5

Did the exercise increase student involvement and action in the lesson?
_____
_____

Did the information about the author and their background invite active questions and discussion by the students?
_____
_____

Did the students see the relationship between today's class activities and other classes or courses by other teachers?
_____
_____

Did the students demonstrate how they could apply what they were hearing or discussing in their day-to-day activities?
_____
_____

What would you, the teacher, do differently next time?
_____
_____
_____
_____

Lesson Plan For Incorporating Critical Thinking

Class/week No:_____ Grade Level:_____

Topic of the class:_____

Why this is valuable for the student to understand: WIFM (What's In It For Me).

_____

_____

How the teacher will develop and approach the subject: Lecture/Q&A/summary with exercises to practice application and demo understanding.

_____

_____

Supporting reading material provided the students:

_____

_____

Author:_____

Author's education and experience:_____

Author's reputation and public profile: _____

Questions as the students work the material for the day (The students WIFM):

Why did the author include this material?

_____

How does this material integrate with other material/readings/presentations they have had?

_____

What is the value to the student to learn about this?

_____

How can the student incorporate the material into their daily lives?

_____

How does this material provide a skill they can use to make better choices?

_____

Post-class Evaluation Of The Effectiveness Of The Exercise

On a scale of 1 to 5 how would you rate the overall activity and learning experience for the students (1 being poor or very little, 5 being excellent)?

1   2   3   4   5

Did the exercise increase student involvement and action in the lesson?
_____

_____

Did the information about the author and their background invite active questions and discussion by the students?
_____

_____

Did the students see the relationship between today's class activities and other classes or courses by other teachers?
_____

_____

Did the students demonstrate how they could apply what they were hearing or discussing in their day-to-day activities?
_____

_____

What would you, the teacher, do differently next time?
_____

_____

_____

_____

Lesson Plan For Incorporating Critical Thinking

Class/week No:_____ Grade Level:_____

Topic of the class:_____

Why this is valuable for the student to understand: WIFM (What's In It For Me).

_____

_____

How the teacher will develop and approach the subject: Lecture/Q&A/summary with exercises to practice application and demo understanding.

_____

_____

Supporting reading material provided the students:

_____

_____

Author:_____

Author's education and experience:_____

Author's reputation and public profile: _____

Questions as the students work the material for the day (The students WIFM):

Why did the author include this material?

_____

How does this material integrate with other material/readings/presentations they have had?

_____

What is the value to the student to learn about this?

_____

How can the student incorporate the material into their daily lives?

_____

How does this material provide a skill they can use to make better choices?

_____

Post-class Evaluation Of The Effectiveness Of The Exercise

On a scale of 1 to 5 how would you rate the overall activity and learning experience for the students (1 being poor or very little, 5 being excellent)?

1   2   3   4   5

Did the exercise increase student involvement and action in the lesson?

_____

_____

Did the information about the author and their background invite active questions and discussion by the students?

_____

_____

Did the students see the relationship between today's class activities and other classes or courses by other teachers?

_____

_____

Did the students demonstrate how they could apply what they were hearing or discussing in their day-to-day activities?

_____

_____

What would you, the teacher, do differently next time?

_____

_____

_____

_____

Lesson Plan For Incorporating Critical Thinking

Class/week No:_____ Grade Level:_____

Topic of the class:_____

Why this is valuable for the student to understand: WIFM (What's In It For Me).

_____

_____

How the teacher will develop and approach the subject: Lecture/Q&A/summary with exercises to practice application and demo understanding.

_____

_____

Supporting reading material provided the students:

_____

_____

Author:_____

Author's education and experience:_____

Author's reputation and public profile: _____

Questions as the students work the material for the day (The students WIFM):

Why did the author include this material?

_____

How does this material integrate with other material/readings/presentations they have had?

_____

What is the value to the student to learn about this?

_____

How can the student incorporate the material into their daily lives?

_____

How does this material provide a skill they can use to make better choices?

_____

Post-class Evaluation Of The Effectiveness Of The Exercise

On a scale of 1 to 5 how would you rate the overall activity and learning experience for the students (1 being poor or very little, 5 being excellent)?

1   2   3   4   5

Did the exercise increase student involvement and action in the lesson?

_____

_____

Did the information about the author and their background invite active questions and discussion by the students?

_____

_____

Did the students see the relationship between today's class activities and other classes or courses by other teachers?

_____

_____

Did the students demonstrate how they could apply what they were hearing or discussing in their day-to-day activities?

_____

_____

What would you, the teacher, do differently next time?

_____

_____

_____

_____

Lesson Plan For Incorporating Critical Thinking

Class/week No:_____ Grade Level:_____

Topic of the class:_____

Why this is valuable for the student to understand: WIFM (What's In It For Me).

_____

_____

How the teacher will develop and approach the subject: Lecture/Q&A/summary with exercises to practice application and demo understanding.

_____

_____

Supporting reading material provided the students:

_____

_____

Author:_____

Author's education and experience:_____

Author's reputation and public profile: _____

Questions as the students work the material for the day (The students WIFM):

Why did the author include this material?

_____

How does this material integrate with other material/readings/presentations they have had?

_____

What is the value to the student to learn about this?

_____

How can the student incorporate the material into their daily lives?

_____

How does this material provide a skill they can use to make better choices?

_____

Post-class Evaluation Of The Effectiveness Of The Exercise

On a scale of 1 to 5 how would you rate the overall activity and learning experience for the students (1 being poor or very little, 5 being excellent)?

1   2   3   4   5

Did the exercise increase student involvement and action in the lesson?

_____

_____

Did the information about the author and their background invite active questions and discussion by the students?

_____

_____

Did the students see the relationship between today's class activities and other classes or courses by other teachers?

_____

_____

Did the students demonstrate how they could apply what they were hearing or discussing in their day-to-day activities?

_____

_____

What would you, the teacher, do differently next time?

_____

_____

_____

_____

Lesson Plan For Incorporating Critical Thinking

Class/week No:_____ Grade Level:_____

Topic of the class:_____

Why this is valuable for the student to understand: WIFM (What's In It For Me).

_____

_____

How the teacher will develop and approach the subject: Lecture/Q&A/summary with exercises to practice application and demo understanding.

_____

_____

Supporting reading material provided the students:

_____

_____

Author:_____

Author's education and experience:_____

Author's reputation and public profile: _____

Questions as the students work the material for the day (The students WIFM):

Why did the author include this material?

_____

How does this material integrate with other material/readings/presentations they have had?

_____

What is the value to the student to learn about this?

_____

How can the student incorporate the material into their daily lives?

_____

How does this material provide a skill they can use to make better choices?

_____

Post-class Evaluation Of The Effectiveness Of The Exercise

On a scale of 1 to 5 how would you rate the overall activity and learning experience for the students (1 being poor or very little, 5 being excellent)?

1   2   3   4   5

Did the exercise increase student involvement and action in the lesson?
_____

_____

Did the information about the author and their background invite active questions and discussion by the students?
_____

_____

Did the students see the relationship between today's class activities and other classes or courses by other teachers?
_____

_____

Did the students demonstrate how they could apply what they were hearing or discussing in their day-to-day activities?
_____

_____

What would you, the teacher, do differently next time?
_____

_____

_____

_____

Lesson Plan For Incorporating Critical Thinking

Class/week No:_____ Grade Level:_____

Topic of the class:_____

Why this is valuable for the student to understand: WIFM (What's In It For Me).

_____

_____

How the teacher will develop and approach the subject: Lecture/Q&A/summary with exercises to practice application and demo understanding.

_____

_____

Supporting reading material provided the students:

_____

_____

Author:_____

Author's education and experience:_____

Author's reputation and public profile: _____

Questions as the students work the material for the day (The students WIFM):

Why did the author include this material?

_____

How does this material integrate with other material/readings/presentations they have had?

_____

What is the value to the student to learn about this?

_____

How can the student incorporate the material into their daily lives?

_____

How does this material provide a skill they can use to make better choices?

_____

Post-class Evaluation Of The Effectiveness Of The Exercise

On a scale of 1 to 5 how would you rate the overall activity and learning experience for the students (1 being poor or very little, 5 being excellent)?

1   2   3   4   5

Did the exercise increase student involvement and action in the lesson?
_____

_____

Did the information about the author and their background invite active questions and discussion by the students?
_____

_____

Did the students see the relationship between today's class activities and other classes or courses by other teachers?
_____

_____

Did the students demonstrate how they could apply what they were hearing or discussing in their day-to-day activities?
_____

_____

What would you, the teacher, do differently next time?
_____

_____

_____

_____

Lesson Plan For Incorporating Critical Thinking

Class/week No:_____ Grade Level:_____

Topic of the class:_____

Why this is valuable for the student to understand: WIFM (What's In It For Me).

_____

_____

How the teacher will develop and approach the subject: Lecture/Q&A/summary with exercises to practice application and demo understanding.

_____

_____

Supporting reading material provided the students:

_____

_____

Author:_____

Author's education and experience:_____

Author's reputation and public profile: _____

Questions as the students work the material for the day (The students WIFM):

Why did the author include this material?

_____

How does this material integrate with other material/readings/presentations they have had?

_____

What is the value to the student to learn about this?

_____

How can the student incorporate the material into their daily lives?

_____

How does this material provide a skill they can use to make better choices?

_____

Post-class Evaluation Of The Effectiveness Of The Exercise

On a scale of 1 to 5 how would you rate the overall activity and learning experience for the students (1 being poor or very little, 5 being excellent)?

1   2   3   4   5

Did the exercise increase student involvement and action in the lesson?

_____

_____

Did the information about the author and their background invite active questions and discussion by the students?

_____

_____

Did the students see the relationship between today's class activities and other classes or courses by other teachers?

_____

_____

Did the students demonstrate how they could apply what they were hearing or discussing in their day-to-day activities?

_____

_____

What would you, the teacher, do differently next time?

_____

_____

_____

_____

Lesson Plan For Incorporating Critical Thinking

Class/week No:_____ Grade Level:_____

Topic of the class:_____

Why this is valuable for the student to understand: WIFM (What's In It For Me).

_____

_____

How the teacher will develop and approach the subject: Lecture/Q&A/summary with exercises to practice application and demo understanding.

_____

_____

Supporting reading material provided the students:

_____

_____

Author:_____

Author's education and experience:_____

Author's reputation and public profile: _____

Questions as the students work the material for the day (The students WIFM):

Why did the author include this material?

_____

How does this material integrate with other material/readings/presentations they have had?

_____

What is the value to the student to learn about this?

_____

How can the student incorporate the material into their daily lives?

_____

How does this material provide a skill they can use to make better choices?

_____

Post-class Evaluation Of The Effectiveness Of The Exercise

On a scale of 1 to 5 how would you rate the overall activity and learning experience for the students (1 being poor or very little, 5 being excellent)?

1   2   3   4   5

Did the exercise increase student involvement and action in the lesson?

_____

_____

Did the information about the author and their background invite active questions and discussion by the students?

_____

_____

Did the students see the relationship between today's class activities and other classes or courses by other teachers?

_____

_____

Did the students demonstrate how they could apply what they were hearing or discussing in their day-to-day activities?

_____

_____

What would you, the teacher, do differently next time?

_____

_____

_____

_____

www.ingramcontent.com/pod-product-compliance
Lightning Source LLC
Chambersburg PA
CBHW080602030426
42336CB00019B/3300